THE WINGS OF WORSHIP

A Course
In Worship

BY KENNETH R. BURCHAM

C.S.S Publishing Co., Inc.
Lima, Ohio

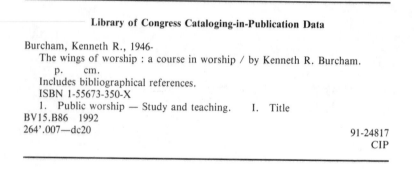

Library of Congress Cataloging-in-Publication Data

Burcham, Kenneth R., 1946-
    The wings of worship : a course in worship / by Kenneth R. Burcham.
      p.   cm.
    Includes bibliographical references.
    ISBN 1-55673-350-X
    1. Public worship — Study and teaching.   I. Title
BV15.B86 1992
264'.007—dc20
                                  91-24817
                                      CIP

9213 / ISBN 1-55673-350-X

To Nancy,
my loving companion
and partner on the journey,
and to our children Cristy,
Lee Ann, Holly, Aaron and Amber.

Acknowledgments

The completion of this final document must begin with an expression of thanks to those who have been of help along the way.

The dedication is to my wife Nancy and our five children, who have given me the time away from home to pursue my journey of faith in the Doctor of Ministry program.

It is with deep gratitude that I express appreciation to Mr. and Mrs. C. Cree Gable for their encouragement and assistance along the way.

Neither the project associates nor I will be the same, because of this experiment in ministry. They gave of their time and of themselves. To them I express thanks.

To Harriett Miller, my advisor and retired professor from United Theological Seminary, I express a deep appreciation for her kindness and work above and beyond the call of duty.

To my consulting faculty I give thanks for the generous time they gave to my project and for their enthusiasm for its advancement. Thank you to Dr. Joseph Goetz, Dr. Geoffrey Lilburne, and Dr. Kendall McCabe.

My regional group was a source of testing and support. There was a determined effort not to let less than one's best pass through the group.

Dr. Mary Olson, director of the Doctor of Ministry program, facilitated the Cincinnati regional for most of my work. She has been supportive and a source of encouragement throughout the program, as has Dr. Howard Snyder, the new Cincinnati regional seminar facilitator.

I want to give thanks to my present church, the College Corner United Methodist Church, for giving me the space and time to complete the writing of this thesis. Moving to the College Corner United Methodist Church in September 1988 from the Rockdale United Methodist Church after completion of the implementation in May 1988 prolonged the journey of writing.

I wish to express my thanks to Diana Hoy for her gift of time and expertise in proofreading this document.

To one and all I express my deepest appreciation.

The final paper is mine. I own the weaknesses and applaud the contribution of those named above, as well as the others who have not been named, but have helped in many different ways.

Kenneth R. Burcham
January 1989

Table Of Contents

Foreword

The Protestant principle of the priesthood of all believers is closely tied to the root meaning of liturgy, "the work of the people." All too often these terms have been interpreted privatistically, on a "do what you like" level which finally ends up as permission to do nothing!

To be a priest means to be actively involved in the offering of worship on behalf of the community. In the priesthood of all believers we are offering our worship not only for but also with our brothers and sisters. We are the doers of worship, not the receivers of it. A Christian congregation is not a group of people who sit passively waiting to be educated or entertained.

This means then that we need to know what we are about in the work of public worship. How is priesthood exercised by the person in the pew? How can the ancient signs and symbols be a means of renewal for the present age? What are the different roles of the baptized general ministry and the ordained representative ministry? What place does the Bible have in the planning of weekly worship? Just as other jobs have their specialized vocabulary, so does the work of worship, the work of the people.

This book, *The Wings Of Worship,* can be a great help in introducing congregations to an understanding of the people's role in public worship. It is simply designed for ease of use in small groups, and it invites and respects the opinions and observations of the participants. Dr. Burcham has designed this study on the basis of his years of pastoral ministry and his conviction that the offering of worship should be the result of an informed collaboration between pastor and people. For those who may be uncertain about how to get this partnership underway, I recommend *The Wings Of Worship.*

Dr. Kendall Kane McCabe
Professor of Preaching and Worship
United Theological Seminary
Dayton, Ohio

Introduction

Welcome to *The Wings Of Worship*, a course designed to bring about worship in one accord in the Sunday morning worship service.

We are working under the assumption that worship in one accord is a goal for which to strive, and that it is attainable through education, discussion and participation of clergy and laity.

In a time when many people come only to the Sunday morning worship, it becomes increasingly important to worship in one accord. The "Church Invisible" is more the "Church Visible" at that time than at any other time.

Through our learning process we may find it necessary to modify our present form of worship. May God help us to be willing!

Lesson 1
Overview

Opening Activities

1. Prayer

2. Sing "O Magnify the Lord"

3. Group activity. The idea here is to cause confusion in getting the group to a desired goal. One possibility is to say we are going to move as a group to such and such a place by using directions prepared for us. Cut enough papers (ahead of time) for everyone to have one. Write directions that will confuse the group process, such as: take two steps forward and one step back; take one step to the left and one to the right; take three steps forward and turn around and take three steps backward or to keep circling around one person. Draw the comparison to a congregation of people worshiping in their own way.

4. Take five minutes and write an order of worship for the Sunday morning service. Please place your name on it so it can be passed back to you at the end of the course so that you can use it as a basis for comparison to see if any of your ideas have changed. Remember, this is to be your order of worship.

Information

The purpose of this course is to help bring one accord in worship in the Sunday morning worship service through education, discussion and participation of clergy and laity.

Worship is declaring the worth of God. Corporate worship is what a group of people do while they are gathered to declare the worth of God (for us that group is a group of Christians). That gathering usually occurs in a place that is considered to be sacred, such as a church, but it does not have to be. The expressions of that worthiness take the form of praise and thanks to God, hearing and proclaiming the Word of God, and administering and receiving the sacraments (communion and baptism).

What is done by means of form and practice is called the liturgy. The liturgy of a congregation is its way of doing worship. It is the forms and practices which are used to give direction and order and meaning to the service.

The value of the liturgy is not as to whether it is formal, informal, structured or free, but it is in the fact that it is an accepted pattern that helps the corporate body to express the worthiness of God (to praise God). It is a highway with entrance ramps for the individual to enter into the flow of traffic, the flow of corporate worship. It is a means by which the individual and corporate body may wing their flight to celestial glory.

The best worship service for a particular gathered group of people is what helps that group of people to declare the worth of God. The forms must have meaning to those who are present. They must not raise barriers. A common language of worship must be spoken. As one person cannot speak two languages at once, but must choose a common language to communicate in a group, we must seek a common language of worship in a group in order to dialogue and commune with God and each other because it is corporate.

The question, then, becomes: "Will the form enable the corporate body to worship?" That being the case, there are cultural factors to be considered in worship. The type and amount of participation in liturgical celebrations using the symbols of faith — and the use of music are always influenced by the social customs of the local setting. It is, therefore, essential to relate the style of liturgy to the nature of the congregation.

Biblical and historical understandings also influence the cultural factors. The present is a product of the past. Sometimes, the present is a reaction to the past but, it is, nonetheless, influenced by the past.

Worship is anamnestic (bringing the past into the present) and proleptic (bringing the future into the present). It is corporate dialogue and communion with God by word, sacrament (baptism and communion), rite, song, prayer and silence.

The God who is worshiped is imminent (present and operating within creation) and transcendent (above and beyond creation, apart from the material universe). That God became flesh in Jesus Christ and is in our midst as we gather in Jesus' name: "For where two or three come together in my name, there am I with them (Matthew 18:20, NIV)."

Worship is to be done "in spirit and in truth (John 4:24, NIV)." That is, worship is to come from the inner being of humanity. Worship is not a posture, although postures are helpful. Worship is not a place, although places can be helpful or harmful. Worship comes from within humanity, the inner being; it is ascribing worthiness to God.

The church is that place where the people of God encourage one another, learn about God, receive the sacraments (baptism and communion) — not the only place, but a special place consecrated for that. It is the place where the Word of God is in creative tension with the people of God and is experienced through the preaching, singing, praying, praising, sacraments, discipling and the fellowshiping.

Corporate worship is most effective when it is done in one accord — that is, when people are gathered worshiping God from within, allowing the liturgy to be the entrance ramp to the highway of praise. When the disciples were gathered together on the day of Pentecost, the Holy Spirit came on them and the church was born. They were in one accord. The liturgy is most effective when it invites the full participation of all present. It invites the full participation when it is understood or, at least, accepted as worship.

Corporate worship is the corporate declaration of the worthiness of God. It is dialogue and communion with oneself, with God, and with others. The liturgy, what is done in public to worship, is best when those present understand it and enter into one accord — oneness of mind and spirit. It is a vehicle to enhance that dialogue and communion. It may vary from local setting to local setting, or even from service to service. Cultural factors, biblical and historical understandings, and traditions are to be considered in creating the particular liturgies.

The liturgy may consist of the word and table (communion and Scripture reading and preaching) at every worship service or may consist of communion alone, or a service of the word. However, it must be done in "spirit and in truth." The key is the worship of God from the inner being.

Discussion Questions

1. **What is your personal goal in worship?**
2. **What is the church?**
3. **What are some of the cultural factors that influence our worship?**
4. **What are some biblical and historical factors that influence our worship?**
5. **What are your expectations of the worship service?**

Evaluations

Have course participants complete the weekly evaluation form from page 63 (you may make copies) and hand it in at the end of the class period.

Lesson 2
Traditional Worship

Opening Activities

1. **Prayer**

2. **Sing "Kum Ba Yah"**

3. **From where do you think our present form of worship came?**

Information

Christian worship arose from Hebrew tradition and worship. Jesus and his early followers were of Hebrew descent. It is, therefore, important to take a look at the influence of this rich heritage.

The major influences were the temple, the synagogue, and the home. The service of the Word has its beginnings in the tabernacle and the temple. Hebrew family worship was the training ground of the youth.

When the temple was destroyed at the time of the Babylonian captivity, Israel faced the civil and theological on its own. However, a complete record of the liturgical development of the church does not exist. The record is very sketchy. There is clear evidence that worship existed. In fact, Scripture says that the early church gathered and worshiped in the temple (Acts 2:46; 3:1). We do not have any formal liturgies, but we do have some liturgical fragments: the *Magnificat* (Luke 1:46-55), *Benedictus* (Luke 1:68-79), *Nunc Dimittus* (Luke 2:29-32), *Hymn of Kenosis* (Philippians 2:6-11), and a possible eucharistic (communion) sermon (John 6:35-50).

This brings up an interesting problem to those who say that they are going to return to the New Testament form of worship. The problem is that it is not certain what the actual practices of the early church were. We do know that the Holy Spirit did not die nor did the church. The Holy Spirit is always with us to guide us in our worship. The church is first a living organism, not an organization.

We can and, indeed should, return to the Christian Scriptures (New Testament) for theological presuppositions and to gain insight and guidance. It is not a book with prescribed rites and ceremonies, nor the insistence upon the lack of these. The principles are there to be worked out by us in our worship as we offer the offerings of worship.

Two of those principles to be found in the Christian Scriptures are: (1) "in spirit and in truth (John 4:24, NIV)" and (2) "in a fitting and orderly way (1 Corinthians 14:40, NIV)."

An Order Of Sunday Worship

While the people are gathering in the Lord's name, a number of things can be done. This is a time for informal greetings, conversations, announcements, welcoming and many other things.

The greeting is the call to worship. It is greeting in the Lord's name and declaring God's presence in the worship. This is to set the place and time apart for God.

The hymn of praise is to call worshipers together as a unit of praise-giving people. This hymn ought to be objective, that is, it should focus on God and not the experience of humanity. (Hymns interspersed in the service were a later development of the church.)

The opening prayer(s) could be the prayer of the day, confession and pardon, or a litany (prayer where the congregation makes the same or almost the same brief response). A responsive prayer is also proper, as is a collect (a short prayer with an address, descriptive clause, petition, result and conclusion). (Prayers were a part of the synagogue worship.)

18

The act of praise is optional. If the prayer is confession and pardon, the act of praise is for forgiveness — the "In Excelsis Deo" could be used. The Gloria Patri is not used as well here as at the conclusion of a psalm. The call to worship could be followed by a psalm which could be followed by the Gloria Patri. (Praise was a part of the synagogue service.)

The prayer of illumination is optional. It is the invocation of blessing of the Holy Spirit on the Word. More than one prayer is not needed. If there is an opening prayer, a prayer of illumination is not necessary although we certainly want illumination.

The Scripture lesson is read for the people to hear the Word of God. It is read and not recited. Recitation is a preaching device and should be saved for later. At the end of the reading the reader can also say, "This is the Word of the Lord," to which the congregation can respond, "Thanks be to God." (The law and the prophets were read as a part of the synagogue service.)

The psalm is a response to the reading of the Word: a metrical form of the psalm is very appropriate. The psalm is optional at this point.

Another Scripture lesson is optional. If a psalm is read or sung, it may be wise not to have another lesson here.

A hymn or song related to the Scriptures of the day or an alleluia may be sung.

The gospel lesson was read to a standing congregation in the early church. This is most certainly still appropriate.

Of course, the sermon is God's message through the speaker to those present. One or more of the Scripture lessons is interpreted. (The synagogue service also had a sermon.)

The response to the Word may include many things. A hymn of invitation or response is very appropriate. This is a proper time for confirmation, baptism, reaffirmation, reception into membership and a creed.

Concerns and prayers, a time for brief intercessions, petitions and thanksgiving, may be prayed by the leader or spontaneously by members of the congregation — a litany of prayer or pastoral prayer may be offered here. Confession and pardon may be done here when there has not been one earlier. The leader leads the people to confession of sin and declares that God has forgiven.

The peace is the people offering one another signs of recognition and love. It may be a handshake, or a "holy kiss." It may involve the exchange, "The peace of the Lord be with you," with the reply, "And also with you."

The offering, which is a sign of commitment, can be received here as a response to the Word of God.

If there is to be no eucharist (communion which takes the place of the animal in the temple), a prayer of thanksgiving, a hymn and dismissal and blessing can be offered at this time.

The benediction is a statement to the people with God's blessing (people are looking up at the leader). It was a part of the synagogue service.

The basic service of the Word (service without the eucharist) comes to us from the daily office (prayer service) of the monastic orders. The sermon, offering and hymns were added to the service later.

Conclusion

Our present understanding of worship is influenced by the Hebrew tradition and the practices of the early church. Let us recognize and build on that history. However, let us never be bound to a form. We must remember that the form is the vehicle.

Discussion Questions

1. How do we train our youth?
2. What do you think was included in New Testament worship?
3. What is the difference between the church and a civic club?

4. What are the Hebrew influences on our forms of worship?
5. What are two guidelines for New Testament worship?

Evaluations

Have course participants complete the weekly evaluation form from page 63 (you may make copies) and hand it in at the end of the class period.

Notes

Lesson 3
Liturgical Year

Opening Activities

1. **Prayer**

2. **"Alleluia" (chorus)**

3. **What is the liturgical year (church year)? Obtain materials of different colors (such as construction paper or posterboard or different symbols and ask the students what these mean to them.**

4. **Share with the group a specific memorable event from your past.**

Information

The church year is divided into times of special seasons as a witness to the historical happenings of the church to remind us of what we are about and for us to remember as present reality (anamnestically). Recent scholarship of Thomas Talley challenges the traditional understanding of the origin of the liturgical year.

Advent is the beginning of the church year. It is a season of four Sundays. It begins on the Sunday closest to November 30, St. Andrew's Day. Its observance began in France during the fourth century. The season varied from four to seven weeks until the Bishop of Rome in the sixth century set the time of four weeks.

The word Advent consists of two Latin words: ad venire, "to come," and means that God in Christ is coming into the world. The coming may be a past experience, a present experience or a future experience.

23

The message of Advent is to prepare. If we are prepared, his coming means salvation, but if we are not prepared, it means judgment. We are to prepare by repentance, prayer and patience.

The mood of Advent is expressed in the color of violet because it gives a feeling of quiet dignity, royalty and repentance. Violet was the traditional color of the robes of a king, which makes it fitting for the coming "King of kings." Advent is a time to think about and repent of sins. It is a time for watching, praying and waiting for our Lord to come again. Blue has recently become an alternate color for Advent because it is a color of hope.

The Christmas season begins with the nativity of our Lord (Christmas Eve and Christmas). The first Sunday after Christmas may be celebrated on December 25 when it falls on a Sunday, and the Christmas lectionary readings (a planned series of readings is the definition of a lectionary) have been used on Christmas Eve.

Epiphany is the oldest season of the church year next to Easter. It falls on January 6. It was a time of celebration of the birth and baptism of Jesus. The festival was divided when December was selected as the birthday of Jesus. The church in the East continued to celebrate Epiphany in terms of the baptism of Jesus while the western church observed the visit of the magi. We now observe the visit of the magi on Epiphany Day and the baptism of Jesus on the first Sunday after Epiphany.

In spite of the fact that Epiphany Day is a major festival like Christmas and Pentecost, many churches ignore January 6 as the Day of Epiphany because it falls on a week day most of the time. Roman Catholics are obligated to attend mass on Epiphany. Epiphany means "manifestation" — Jesus the Light of God manifests the glory of God. It has been known by other names throughout history: "feast of the manifestation," "feast of the three kings" and "the twelfth day."

The Sundays after January 6 are called Sunday after Ephiphany. The number of weeks it is observed depends on the date of Easter. It covers from six to nine Sundays.

The colors vary. White is used for three of the Sundays: Epiphany Day, the Baptism of our Lord (Epiphany 1) and the Transfiguration of our Lord (the last Sunday before Lent).

The Lenten season is the time of spiritual preparation through repentance and growth in our walk with God in anticipation for Easter. This is when the passion and death of Jesus come into our view. It begins on a special day of repentance, Ash Wednesday, and ends in the depth of sorrow and tragedy of Good Friday. The word comes from an old Anglo-Saxon word *Lencten* or *Lenchten* which means the lengthening of the days. It is a period of 40 days.

Sundays were never a part of Lent, so we speak of "Sundays in Lent" not "of Lent." The last days of Lent or Holy Week and events observed are Palm Sunday — entry of our Lord into Jerusalem; Monday — cleansing of the temple; Tuesday — the discourse on the Mount of Olives; Wednesday — Judas' agreement; Maundy Thursday — final supper of Jesus with his disciples; Good Friday — crucifixion; and Saturday — the rest in the tomb.

The traditional color for Lent and Holy Week is purple (except for Good Friday). An alternative color for Ash Wednesday is black because of the repentance of the Christian in which he is to die to self. White is a suggested possibility for Maundy Thursday to celebrate the beginning of the Lord's supper. During Holy Week, red is suggested in place of purple to remind people of the sacrifice of our Lord. In place of black on Good Friday, it is suggested as a possibility that a deeper shade of red be used than that used during Holy Week to reflect the shed blood of our Lord.

The next season is the Easter season. The name Easter is the adaption of the name *Eastre* which was the name of a Teutonic goddess of spring and dawn. The original name for Easter was *Pascha*, a Hebrew word for Passover. The day has been known as "the Lord's day of resurrection" and "Paschal day of the resurrection."

Christians are still not agreed about the date for Easer. The Council of Nicea in A.D. 325 declared Easter to be "on the first Sunday after the full moon on or after the first day of spring, March 21, or if the full moon is on Sunday, the next Sunday after." Therefore, Easter can fall between March 22 and April 25.

Easter is the highest of days for the Christian church. Our Sunday worship is in recognition of the resurrection of Jesus. It is a time of joy, of celebration of eternal life, of newness of life, of future hope and of victory. The color is white. Gold may be used as an alternative color.

The season is a season of 50 days. It opens on Easter Day and runs through Pentecost Day. We speak of "Sundays of Easter." Other festival days and seasons of the church depend upon the date of Easter.

Pentecost is observed as a festival and as a season. It is the anniversary of the coming of the Holy Spirit upon the disciples and the birth of the church. The word comes from the greek, *pentekoste,* which means "50" and refers to 50 days after Easter. It is also referred to as "Whitsunday," which is a contraction of "White Sunday." It was called such because candidates for baptism and confirmation wore white robes to symbolize that they were cleansed by the Holy Spirit.

The color of the Day of Pentecost is red because it is the color of fire — the Spirit came as tongues of fire (Acts chapter 2). The fire represents God. Red also stands for the blood of the martyrs. The color for the Sundays after Pentecost is green, which stands for growth, because disciples are to grow in the Spirit. Trinity Sunday is the first Sunday after Pentecost, in which the Trinity is celebrated. The last Sunday after Pentecost and the Sunday before Advent begins is Christ the King Sunday.

The Church Year

Advent — always includes four Sundays and begins on Sunday, November 27, or the first Sunday after November 27, and lasts until sunset on December 24. The color of Advent is purple or blue.

Christmas Season — sunset December 24 through Epiphany Day (January 6). The color is white on Christmas Eve, Christmas Day and on the first and second Sundays after Christmas. Epiphany Day and/or the first Sunday in January is white.

Season after Epiphany — is from January 7 through the day before Lent (day before Ash Wednesday). The color on the first Sunday after Epiphany (Baptism of the Lord Sunday) and last Sunday after Epiphany (Transfiguration Sunday) is white. Green is the color for the second through the next-to-last Sunday.

Lent is from the seventh Wednesday before Easter to sunset Easter Eve.

Color: Ash Wednesday (first day of Lent) — purple or black.

First through fifth Sunday in Lent — purple.

Passion/Palm Sunday (sixth Sunday in Lent) — purple or white.

Monday, Tuesday and Wednesday in Holy Week — purple or red.

Maundy Thursday — purple or red.

Good Friday — black or a deeper shade of red.

Holy Saturday — no color.

Easter Season — is from sunset Easter Eve through the Day of Pentecost.

Color: Easter Eve and Easter Day — white.

Second through sixth Sunday of Easter — white.

Ascension Day (sixth Thursday of Easter) — white.

Seventh Sunday of Easter or Ascension Sunday — white.

Day of Pentecost or the eighth Sunday of Easter — red.

Season after Pentecost — is from the day after Pentecost through the day before Advent.

Color: First Sunday after Pentecost, or Trinity Sunday — white.

Second through next-to-last Sunday after Pentecost — green.

All Saints' Day, November 1, or All Saints' Sunday (First Sunday in November) — white.

Last Sunday after Pentecost, or Christ the King — white.

The Basic Colors — White or gold represent festive occasions.

Purple is the color of penitence and royalty.

Red is the color of fire and blood.

Green is the color of growth.

Paraments And Vestments

The *paraments* (hangings of cloth which decorate the Lord's table, pulpit and lectern if present) should be in colors that signify the season or day of the church year and adorned with symbols that show various parts of the Christian faith.

Those in leadership roles may wear robes. Two very common robes are the academic robe and the alb. The academic robe, which traditionally was black but can now be found in various colors, came from the academic dress of medieval universities and was the uniform of scholars. It can be worn with a hood that indicates the wearer's degree. If the wearer has a doctor's degree, it may have three sleeve stripes. The alb is the oldest Christian vestment and was part of the everyday dress of Roman men and women. After it passed out of style, it continued to be used as a worship vestment. The alb is usually white or off-white.

Stoles, a badge of ordination, indicate the one who has been called to lead the community in the sacramental life of the church. Stoles are long narrow bands over the shoulders and down in the front to about the knees. They are worn with the academic robe and the alb and should also be in the color of the season of the church year.

Keeping time with the liturgical (church) year is one way of preaching the whole gospel and sharing with our brothers and sisters in Christ the heritage of Jesus Christ. It also provides a worship space which is more colorful and meaningful in its appearance.

Discussion Questions

1. Where does summer fit into the church year?
2. What are some symbols that you can think of? The wedding ring is a symbol.
3. How does keeping time with the liturgical year preach the whole gospel?
4. Does the presence of paraments, vestments and symbols coordinated with the colors of the church year add meaning to your worship experience?
5. Should we follow the church year? Why? Why not?

Evaluations

Have course participants complete the weekly evaluation form from page 63 (you may make copies) and hand it in at the end of the class period.

Notes

Lesson 4
Dividing The Church

Opening Activities

1. Prayer

2. Sing "They'll Know We Are Christians by Our Love"

3. Does denominationalism foster love?

Information

The one accord that existed on the Day of Pentecost did not last very long. Unfortunately, the church is marked by a history of division. In this lesson we are going to take a look at some of that history.

The persecution under the Roman Empire that began in 64 A.D. under Nero ended in 313, when Christianity was legalized by the Edict of Milan. It became the sole and official state religion in 395 A.D.

Papal power was not really established until the sixth century A.D., even though the history of the Roman Catholic popes date back to Peter (the Petrine doctrine taught that the Roman church had been established by Peter and that subsequent bishops of Rome would control all other dioceses).

Two main branches of the church developed: the western branch, with its headquarters in Rome, and the eastern branch, with its headquarters in Constantinople (Istanbul, Turkey). The two branches became formally divided around 1,000 A.D. The Eastern branch became the Eastern Orthodox or Greek Church; and the western branch became known as the Roman Catholic Church.

The years 590 to 1517 A.D. are known as the Middle Ages. It is during this time that the church was the all-powerful place for learning and civilization in the underdeveloped lands of Europe. Many monasteries and convents were built and they became centers of scholarship and devotion to God.

The Crusades, dating from about 1100 to 1300 A.D., were launched in an attempt to get the Holy Land back from the Muslims. Indulgences (doing away with purgatorial punishment for past sins) were being sold.

The papacy in Rome grew in power, extending into a vast and wealthy papal empire far greater than any secular monarchy, in sharp contrast to the poverty and simplicity of the followers of religious orders. The veneration of Mary, the mother of Jesus, had been growing in popularity.

The common folk felt alienated from an extravagant and self-satisfied church. Religion became a set of rules to escape punishment rather than a joyful experience.

In Germany a young man named Martin Luther became a Roman Catholic priest with a doctorate in theology. Luther became increasingly disturbed about some of the things the church was doing. He wanted to debate things with the leaders of the church. Therefore, in 1517, he nailed 95 topics, or theses, to the church door in Wittenberg. (The church door was a kind of community bulletin board.)

The moveable type, press, ink and paper that had been invented shortly before Luther's time made it possible for his theses and other writings to be printed and spread throughout Germany and nearby countries. Many people agreed with him and began to demand reforms in the Roman Catholic Church. Since they protested, they were called "Protestants." Luther was excommunicated from the church in 1521 A.D.

The Council of Trent (1545-1563) brought about some of the needed reform in the Roman Catholic Church.

Luther's writings were used by God to awaken John Calvin, a Frenchman. Calvin lived at the same time as Luther, but he worked in France and Geneva, Switzerland. Calvin's teaching was the foundation of the protestant churches known as Reformed: Baptists, Presbyterians and many non-denominational churches.

In England, the Roman Catholic Church broke apart in 1534 A.D. The English king was named head of the Anglican Church (Church of England). Methodism arose from the Anglican Church in the 1700s.

From 1738 to 1791, John Wesley rode over England and Ireland preaching and teaching Jesus Christ, establishing a group called Methodists.

Some of these Methodists from England and Ireland came to America in the 1760s. To minister to them, John Wesley sent preachers from England. One became the "John Wesley of the New World" — Francis Asbury, who arrived in America in 1771.

Anglicans returned to England during the American Revolution, but Francis Asbury stayed. On December 24, 1784, American Methodism, or the Methodist Episcopal Church, was established.

Philip William Otterbein, friend of Francis Asbury, and Martin Boehm formed what became the United Brethren Church. Otterbein and Asbury believed alike on many things, but Otterbein wanted to maintain his Reformed church status.

John Albright, a Pennsylvania farmer, was influential in establishing the Evangelical Association. However, in 1891 some left to form the United Evangelical Church (even Paul and Barnabas separated over whether to take John Mark, in Act 15). They came back together in 1922, forming the Evangelical Church, which joined together with the United Brethren Church in 1946 to from the Evangelical United Brethren Church.

In 1968 the Evangelical United Brethren Church joined the Methodists to form the United Methodist Church.

The Methodists have had their splits also. The Methodist Episcopal Church in 1844 split over the issue of slavery into the Methodist Episcopal Church and the Methodist Episcopal Church, South. They united once again in 1939, forming the Methodist Church. This also included the Methodist Protestant Church which had left the Methodist Episcopal Church in 1830.

Discussion Questions

1. Are denominations important?
2. Are there valid reasons for splits?
3. What about the love mentioned in 1 John 2:9-11?
4. What bearing does Romans 8:28 have on this subject?

Evaluations

Have course participants complete the weekly evaluation form from page 63 (you may make copies) and hand it in at the end of the class period.

Lesson 5
Tools Of Worship

Opening Activities

1. **Prayer**

2. **Sing "The Church's One Foundation"**

3. **How important are the architecture and the furnishings? How important were they in the tabernacle (Exodus 25-27)?**

Information

The space in which we worship is important, because it influences what happens as we worship. The material things are there to help us express inwardly what they suggest outwardly. The room for worship is often referred to as the sanctuary.

There is usually a hallway, or vestibule or lobby between the outer door and the inner door of the sanctuary, which is called the narthex. This serves to keep distractions to a minimum when people come in late and to allow for needed preparations before entering the sanctuary.

The rooms designed for worship (sanctuaries) differ in many ways, but they are normally designed to draw one's attention to a certain focal area. That focal area which is usually on a raised level is commonly called the chancel. The place where the congregation sits is called the nave.

Sometimes the chancel end of the sanctuary is referred to as the east, the rear of the nave as the west, the left as the north and the right side as the south, because churches traditionally were built facing the east, the direction of the rising sun, which is a sign of the resurrection.

The chancel traditionally contains at least three key furnishings: a table, a pulpit and a baptismal font.

The table is known as the Lord's table, altar table, holy table, communion table or altar. It symbolizes God's presence and is the symbolic center of the life of the church.

The pulpit is a stand from which the minister delivers the message and conducts other parts of the service. Sometimes a lectern is present and is used for readings and conducting other parts of the service.

A baptismal font is present for use in baptism. In some denominations the font is at the entrance to the nave because baptism is seen as the entrance into the church. Sometimes a baptistry is present, where persons can be immersed.

Often the chancel area contains seats for the chior and a piano and an organ. There is often a rail around or inside the chancel area so that people can kneel for prayer, communion or commitment. This rail can be called the altar rail or communion rail.

The pulpit-centered pattern consists of a raised platform with the pulpit in the center. The communion table is usually in front of the pulpit on a lower level. There is no lectern. The baptismal font can be found in various locations.

The divided chancel is a second type of arrangement. The focal point is a table or altar centered against the wall. The pulpit is on one side of the chancel and the lectern or baptismal font is on the other side. Some churches with this type have put in a free-standing Lord's table for communion purposes.

The free-standing Lord's table in an open space with the pulpit to one side is often balanced on the other side by the baptismal font.

The appearance of the chancel can reinforce the message if it is properly arranged. On the other hand, if it is not properly cared for, it can make it very difficult to hear what is said. Remember, the material things are there to help express internally what they say externally.

The chancel is also furnished with various other items of a practical and a symbolic nature.

It is customary that there be a large symbol of Christ near the communion table. It is usually a cross. It ought to be large enough that it draws attention to itself without detracting from the communion table. It should not be on the table. The cross on the communion table is of medieval origin. A small cross was placed by the priest on the altar as an object of private devotion, but it was invisible to the congregation.

Candles have been used in Christian worship since early times. They were used at first to provide light for reading, but of late they continue in use to symbolize that Christ is the light of the world (John 8:12; 12:46).

The Paschal candle is a large decorative candle which is symbolic of Christ's appearances following the resurrection. The candle is lighted at the Easter vigil (Easter Eve or the first service of Easter) and carried in procession to a place near the Lord's table where it remains until the Day of Pentecost. It is lighted at each service until the Day of Pentecost. It is then placed near the baptismal font and lighted whenever there is a baptism. It is sometimes carried at the head of a funeral procession.

Some churches have eternal lights, sanctuary lamps, which are suspended from the ceiling or mounted on the wall near the communion table. These burn continuously. In the Roman Catholic Church tradition they represent the presence of Christ in the reserved sacrament, but in Protestant tradition they represent the presence of Christ in the church.

Candle lighters and extinguishers, used to light and extinguish the candles, should match or coordinate with the candlesticks.

Offering plates are often bought to coordinate with the altarware. When the offering is brought forward during the service, the plates are often received at the altar and stacked in a matching receiving basis. Empty plates are not to be placed on the altar. Plates with money can be placed on the altar if they do not detract from the primary function of the table as the place where communion takes place.

An open Bible placed on the communion table detracts from the function of the table. It confuses the function of the pulpit with that of the table. It is, therefore, better to have it on the pulpit.

Flowers should not be placed on the Lord's table, because they detract from the primary purpose of the table, which is the place where communion is celebrated. Since flowers symbolize the resurrection, no type of artificial flowers are appropriate for the worship environment.

The principle for worship furnishings and altarware is integrity. The worship environment is to reinforce the integrity of the gospel.

Discussion Questions

1. Should the open Bible be put on our communion table?
2. Should we use artificial flowers?

Evaluations

Have course participants complete the weekly evaluation form from page 63 (you may make copies) and hand it in at the end of the class period.

Lesson 6
Creeds And Prayers

Opening Activities

1. Prayer

2. Sing "I'll Tell the World That I'm a Christian"

3. Repeat in unison the Apostles Creed

4. Are creeds important?

Information

Creeds are summaries of basic beliefs and are used in worship and in teachings. The word creed is derived from the Latin *credo*, "I believe," and signifies a confession of faith, articles of belief. Creeds grow from within the church. They are conclusions to which the church has come in its understanding of the Word of God and in its defense against errors.

The three ecumenical creeds (unifying creeds) preserve for us the substance of the faith of the church: (1) the Apostles' Creed; (2) the Nicene Creed; and (3) the Athanasian Creed.

The Apostles' Creed is an expansion of the baptismal confession. It is a statement of faith, a summary of the facts. It was not written by the apostles, but gets its name from the fact that it represents their teachings. In the early church some form of belief had to be confessed for admission into the society of believers.

In its final form, the Apostles' Creed is the baptismal creed for the western church. It is dated from 100 to 150 A.D. and is essentially what we have now. It is certain that from

390 A.D. it existed substantially in the same form that we now have. The creed as follows was taken from *Christian Theology*, Volume I, by H. Orton Wiley:

> *I believe in God the Father Almighty, maker of heaven and earth;*
> *And in Jesus Christ his only Son, our Lord; who was conceived by the Holy Ghost, born of the Virgin Mary; suffered under Pontius Pilate; was crucified, dead and buried; he ascended into hell; the third day he rose again from the dead; he ascended into heaven, and sitteth on the right hand of God the Father Almighty; from thence he shall come to judge the quick and the dead.*
> *I believe in the Holy Ghost; the Holy Catholic Church; the communion of saints; the forgiveness of sins; the resurrection of the body; and the life everlasting. Amen.*

The Nicene Creed was adopted at the First Ecumenical Council, held at Nicaea at Bythynia in the summer of A.D. 325. The council was called by Emperor Constantine, who was not even a Christian at the time. He had hoped to restore peace to the church, which was distracted by the Arian controversy (saw Christ as the incarnate logos, Word of God but as neither God nor human). The text with a few variations is now universally accepted and is as follows (from *Christian Theology*, Volume I, by H. Orton Wiley):

> *I believe in one God, the Father Almighty, Maker of heaven and earth, and of all things visible and invisible.*
> *And in one Lord Jesus Christ, the only-begotten Son of God; begotten of his Father before all worlds, God of God, Light of light, Very God of very God, begotten, not made; being of one substance with the Father; by whom all things were made; who for us men and our salvation came down from heaven, and was incarnate by the Holy Ghost of the Virgin Mary, and was made man; and was crucified also for us under Pontius Pilate; he suffered and was buried; and the third day he arose again*

according to the Scriptures; and ascended into heaven;
and sitteth on the right hand of the Father; and he shall
come again, with glory, to judge both the quick and the
dead: whose kingdom shall have no end.

And I believe in the Holy Ghost, the Lord and Giver
of Life, who proceedeth from the Father and the Son;
who with the Fahter and the Son together is worshiped
and glorified; who spake by the prophets; and I believe
in one Catholic and Apostolic Church; I acknowledge one
baptism for the remission of sins; and I look for the resur-
rection of the dead; and the life of the world to come.
Amen.

The Athanasian Creed is a Latin document with an uncertain date. It is assigned a fifth century date by some and a seventh century date by others. It is a further expansion of the Apostles' Creed and is more specific in its teachings of the trinity and the incarnation. It was not adopted by any council, but was received in the seventh century as an ecumenical symbol. The creed is too long for common use and has been omitted from the Liturgy of the Protestant Episcopal Church of America and will be omitted in our study.

The Chalcedonian Creed was drawn up to correct the various errors and deficiencies in the doctrine of Christ's person. It is still acknowledged as the orthodox statement. The Chalcedonian Council convened in 451 A.D. The creed will be omitted here.

We will now take a look at a more recenlty developed creed. The United Methodist Social Creed (from the 1984 *Book of Discipline*):

We believe in God, Creator of the World; and in Jesus
Christ the Redeemer of creation. We believe in the Holy
Spirit, through whom we acknowledge God's gifts, and
we repent of our sin in misusing these gifts to idolatrous
ends.

We affirm the natural world as God's handiwork and
dedicate ourselves to its preservation, enhancement and
faithful use by humankind.

We joyfully receive, for ourselves and others, the blessings of community, sexuality, marriage and the family.

We commit ourselves to the rights of men, women, children, youth, young adults, the aging and those with handicapping conditions; to improvement of the quality of life; and to the rights and dignity of racial, ethnic, and religious minorities.

We believe in the right and duty of persons to work for the good of themselves and others, and in the protection of their welfare in so doing; in the rights to property as a trust from God, collective bargaining, and responsible consumption; and in the elimination of economic and social distress.

We dedicate ourselves to peace throughout the world, to freedom for all peoples and to the rule of justice and law among nations.

We believe in the present and final triumph of God's Word in human affairs, and gladly accept our commission to manifest the life of the gospel in the world. Amen.[1]

Creeds arise out of the church. They are not forced upon the church. They are usually succinct ways of saying one or a number of things.

Prayer

The God that we confess in Jesus Christ is the same God to whom we pray. Prayer shows our dependence upon God. It is the offering of ourselves to God through the mediation of Jesus the Christ by means of the Holy Spirit (John 14-16). There is prayer that an individual offers and there is prayer that a body of believers gathered together offers, corporate prayer. Since we are concerned with corporate worship, we are concerned about the corporate prayer.

Prayers can be read, said from memory, or said spontaneously, but they must be prayed from the heart. They must express the desire of the heart.

Corporate prayer is the body of Christ together lifting up the needs of individual lives, of the corporate life, of the community life, and of the world. (The Lord's Prayer is corporate.)

The prayer of confession is of no value to us when said in public unless we really mean it. There is need for confession of sin for our part in the failure of the church to do what it should be doing (see Nehemiah, chapter one and his confession for sins in identification with corporate Israel). The absolution is not forgiving sins, but it is announcing the confidence that God who heard the repentant voice has forgiven.

The collect (a short prayer with an address, descriptive clause, petition, result and conclusion) can be prayed in unison or said aloud by a leader followed by the "amen" response of the congregation (which is always the response of the people, not the one praying). The following is an example of a collect:

O God, who knows the secrets of all hearts: Grant
us forgiveness for secret sins, that we be pure and have
your peace within; through Jesus Christ our Lord. Amen.

The pastoral prayer is the leader and congregation praying together, lifting up the needs of the individual, the body of believers, the community and the world. The parts of the pastoral prayer are to be done sometime during the service if not specifically during the prayer: Adoration, confession; thanksgiving for forgiveness; intercessions for the church, the world, the nation and the life of the Immediate Community; local concerns (Aunt Lizzie's gout, etc.); general thanksgiving; and doxological conclusion.

The litany is a prayer in which fixed or nearly the same short responses are made to biddings or petitions of the leader:

Leader: From the curse of war,
People: O Lord, deliver us.
Leader: From believing and speaking lies about nations,
People: O Lord, deliver us.

Another type of prayer is the responsive prayer. In this type of prayer the leader and people alternate in responses in praying, as in the responsive reading.

Unison prayers are sometimes difficult to say, but they are also beneficial and exemplify the corporate nature of prayer.

Creeds and corporate prayers are ways for us to enter into the worship in one accord. They are entrance ramps for us to get on the same highway of praise going in the same direction to declare the worth of God.

Discussions Questions

1. What is the Holy Catholic Church?
2. What common factor or pattern for organization do the Apostles' Creed and the Nicene Creed have?
3. Do you think churches have any business making a social creed?
4. Do you think prayers that are read in a service do any good?
5. Do you think prayers read in unison do any good?

Evaluations

Have course participants complete the weekly evaluation form from page 63 (you may make copies) and hand it in at the end of the class period.

---

[1]"The United Methodist Social Creed" reprinted from *The Book of Discipline of the United Methodist Church,* 1984. Copyright (c) 1984, The United Methodist Publishing House. Reprinted by permission.

Lesson 7
Hymns And Worship

Opening Activities

1. Prayer

2. Sing one or two verses of several favorite hymns such as: "Victory in Jesus," "Amazing Grace," or "The Old Rugged Cross"

3. Why do you like to sing? What is the purpose of singing hymns (Exodus 15:1; Psalms 101:1; 1 Corinthians 14:15)

Information

Music in churches is used as an aid to and part of worship and as entertainment.

Music had a long and important tradition among our Hebrew ancestors. It was used on every public occasion as a form of expression. About 1040 B.C. King David, who was a musician (1 Samuel 16:23), appointed certain of the Levites to provide music for liturgical services (1 Chronicles 14:4-7), and later on is found a listing of the number of services of musicians (1 Chronicles 25). In Hezekiah's reign we find that the Levites still played music for the temple worship (2 Chronicles 29:25). After the Babylonian exile and the restoration of the temple order in Jerusalem, the Levite families resumed that office (Nehemiah 12:35-36, 45-46).

The music in the temple at Jerusalem was very likely elaborate. There was possibly a large choir of Levites and an orchestra composed of many different instruments. The ceremonial trumpets gave fanfares. Because of the fall of

Jerusalem in A.D. 70 and the lack of authentic records, we do not know the exact nature of the music.

The Israelites no doubt had wind instruments (Genesis 4:21), stringed instruments (Psalm 33:2) and percussion instruments (Psalm 150:5).

Greek music had its impact on the early church. Our music heritage has been influenced through many avenues. It came to us through the Roman Christians, who used a borrowed musical idiom from Greek and possibly Jewish chants.

But what is a hymn anyway? It has been defined as "a generic term for any kind of song suited to congregational expression in worship."[1] They may be expressions of belief, of prayer, of personal experience, of exhortation to one another or praise to God.

Technically speaking, the term hymn refers to the text and not the tune. Hymns are poems.

Poems are usually organized into sections of regular and equal structure known as stanzas. A stanza of a hymn consists of a series of lines, while a verse is a line, arranged together in a pattern of meter and rhyme.

In earlier times a hymnbook looked like most other collections of poetry with the words on pages in stanzas. The only references to tunes was the listing of names that could be found elsewhere.

When hymns are matched to tunes, the meter must agree as well as the musical and textual accents. By looking at the metrical index, one can see the tunes that can be interchanged.

A hymn can also be thought to be a poem because of its inner expression and content. The poet Milton said that poetry should be simple, sensuous and passionate. Hymns make use of rhetorical devices and figures of speech such as hyperbole (exaggeration), personification (representing a thing as a person), and many others.

Good hymns are difficult to write. They are a unique form of literary art. In the words of someone else:

> *It may not be as good as superior poetry, but it can have an excellence all its own . . . By contrast the hymn writer*

has to produce something with others in mind, . . . The
hymnist, moreover, is not only speaking to others but on
behalf of others to God. [2]

Hymns can be objective and subjective. The objective hymn turns the attention to God and should be used at the beginning of the worship service. It makes God the focus of attention.

The subjective hymn is a turning of the focus on human beings or on subjective experience. The subjective hymn should come later in the service. Hymns used for altar calls are subjective.

The hymn, therefore, like a good piece of journalism, is clear, memorable and short. It has a bit of heightened imagination, but it gives expression to universal religious truth.

Discussion Questions

1. Do you think it makes any difference as to what type of hymn we use or where we use it?

2. What is your favorite hymn and why? Is it objective or subjective?

Evaluations

Have course participants complete the weekly evaluation form from page 63 (you may make copies) and hand it in at the end of the class period.

---

[1]Harry Eskew and Hugh T. McElrath, *Sing with Understanding* (Nashville: Broadman Press, 1980), p. 7.

[2]*Ibid.,* Eskew and McElrath, p. 24.

Notes

Lesson 8
Ritual And Celebrations

Opening Activities

1. Prayer

2. Sing "O Master, Let Me Walk with Thee"

3. Is ritual important? Is it important in celebration? Should it be? Could it be?

Information

Ritual refers to the prescribed words in an act of worship while a ceremonial refers to the actions (for example, the exchange of marriage vows is part of the ritual while the woman and man facing each other and holding hands is part of the ceremonial).

If words are not important, it does not matter what we say. If actions are not important, it does not matter what we do. Scripture tells us that words are important (Matthew 12:36) and what we do is important (James 2:26; 2:20).

A much admired expression throughout western culture in both sacred and secular circles has been that of "self-giving." That is certainly heightened by the fact that God loved us so much that God sent Jesus (John 3:16). Jesus himself and his words proclaimed the self-giving of God (words and actions).

We are not usually called to give our lives for others, but we give or refuse to give of ourselves in various ways throughout the day. Acts of kindness are forms of self-giving — forms of love. The refusal to do such things is evidence of the lack of love.

Words and actions are ways that we give ourselves. It has been said that actions speak louder than words. Indeed, our actions and words go hand in hand. It is only when the two do not match that we realize that something is wrong. Agreement is a sign of integrity.

Public worship depends constantly on our actions as a means of expressing God's self-giving to us, our self-giving to God and our self-giving to one another. This is not to contrast words and actions. Much of what we do is accompanied by spoken words. Words and actions, or rites and ceremonial, complement each other in worship and in life. Some of our actions are for comfort, such as sitting down during the sermon. Some of our actions are important bearers of meaning, such as bowing our heads during prayer.

Our humanity needs action as an outward and visible sign of self-giving. God knows what our needs are. That is the reason for the sacraments. They are God's self-giving actions to or for us.

We have, somehow, in Protestantism settled for the idea that words are more spiritual than actions. Does not Christ give himself through the words of the sermon as well as the bread and wine? Our humanity depends upon both words and actions for perception in everyday life and in worship.

The quality of celebration is related to the social nature of worship. It is related to the ability of all present to enter the ritual in one accord in word and action to give of themselves. For example, the more who enter into the ritual of receiving members, the better the service. There is no magic in the words alone or in the actions alone, but the power lies in what they both at their best represent: "worship in spirit and in truth."

The sacraments are God's self-giving acts to us. They are sign acts. The words and actions are important at the time of the sacraments.

The words and actions at a funeral are important. For the Christian, death is a celebration. For those who are left behind, it is saying "good-bye!" Yes! There will be reunion later, but this is a temporary good-bye. The funeral is a time for closure with the deceased, for reassurance to the loved ones of victory in Christ, and for celebration of the life of the one who has entered the presence of the Lord. It is the last witness for the deceased. As a Christian, it is the right and privilege of the deceased to have that celebration in the church — preferably with a closed casket covered by a pall. Some choose a memorial, which is fine, but there ought to be a time for family and friends to view the body.

The ritual and ceremonial of the Christian marriage are important. The couple are the ministers of the rite while the pastor or priest presides. The couple marry each other, making a commitment to one another before God. In fact, God is a part of that covenant.

Church membership is a covenant relationship between an individual and a group of people and God.

There is something about going public with commitments and celebrations that makes them a firm part of our life. A ritual is a prescribed way of doing things. What we say is important and what we do is important. Our words and actions need to agree.

Discussion Questions

1. What actions are significant in worship such as bowing the head for prayer?
2. Do you think we need more ritual or less ritual in our services?
3. Can celebration be prescribed?

Evaluations

Have course participants complete the weekly evaluation form from page 63 (you may make copies) and hand it in at the end of the class period.

Notes

Lesson 9
The Sacraments

Opening Activities

1. Prayer

2. Sing "The Church's One Foundation"

3. Are baptism and communion important?

Information

The foundation for the sacrament of baptism and sacrament of the Lord's supper is the creation of the church by Jesus. Participation in these sacraments is mandatory because Jesus commanded it and they are a means of grace.

Baptism is the initiatory means of grace and the eucharist (communion) is an ongoing means of grace. Baptism is God's act of self-giving to humanity. It does not guarantee a life of faith. It is not baptismal regeneration. It is the initiation into the church at whatever age the person is when it is administered. God's Spirit is active in baptism in the initiation and lifelong journey. Baptism and confirmation is, indeed, one act and ought to be handled as such with affirmation, reaffirmation and renewal occurring later and periodically. Unless the Holy Spirit of God is present and active (invited in), there is only form.

When the Holy Spirit is present and active, there is no reason to re-invite that presence again in baptism — regeneration. But there may, indeed, be the need to confess our sins and to ask forgiveness from God for our waywardness, and perhaps to remember our baptism, anamnestically — allowing the spirit of God to be in control in our lives again.

Baptism is an event received as pure gift; no one deserves baptism. The one being baptized is the passive recipient of what God does through the action of others. God incorporates a person into the church through the act of baptism.

There is a unity in water baptism and the gift of the Holy Spirit, but one is not to hold a stopwatch as to the time of God's activity. The human side of baptism is allowing the Spirit to take control — to come in.

Jesus said to baptize. The one who is baptized experiences union with Jesus and his work, incorporation into the church, the gift of the Holy Spirit, the forgiveness of sin and re-birth. It is an action done to me, for me, rather than by me.

The sacrament of the Lord's supper was instituted by the Lord on the night that he was betrayed. Unlike baptism, which is not repeated, the communion is a repeated experience of God's self-giving that Christians observe from baptism until death. The self-giving of God occurs through the bread and the wine.

Communion shows our oneness with Christ and each other. It shows our hope of the return of Christ. It is for those who are members of the Body of Christ regardless of age.

There are those who think that communion ought to be a part of every Sunday morning worship service. They believe that word and table go together to make a worship service. However, it would seem to me that the key is real worship whether you have word and table (service of the Word and communion) or just word or just table. The key is "worship in spirit and in truth."

Jesus did not say to have communion every time we meet, but he did say to do so in remembrance of him. Yes, apparently, the beginning church in Acts had communion daily. At least several of the reformers wanted communion weekly in the worship service. The early Methodists had communion quarterly at the quarterly conferences, where a qualified (ordained) clergy person was present to administer it.

Discussion Questions

1. At what age should a person be baptized? Should infants be baptized?
2. Should a person be rebaptized?
3. How often should we have communion?
4. Let's discuss the baptism and communion rituals.

Evaluations

Have course participants complete the weekly evaluation form from page 63 (you may make copies) and hand it in at the end of the class period.

Notes

Lesson 10
Order Of Worship

Opening Activities

1. **Prayer**

2. **Sing "O Worship the King"**

Information

Today we complete our journey together on the road to one accord in worship through education, discussion and participation by clergy and laity. Even though the course ends with this lesson, let us continue to work toward that one accord. We have learned much, but there is much more to learn. We have experienced much, but there is much more to experience.

We have learned and experienced that worship is declaring the worth of God. That worth is expressed through praise and thanks to God, through hearing and proclaiming the Word of God and through administering and receiving the sacraments of baptism and communion.

The form and practice of what we do when we gather in worship is called the liturgy. It can be formal or informal, but it is still the liturgy. The formality or lack of it is determined by culture, traditions and understandings of the Hebrew and Christian Scriptures.

Denominations have developed because of the different ways of expressing the worth of God. Some divisions have occurred for good reasons and some have not.

The observance of the Christian year, liturgical year, helps to proclaim the whole gospel. It keeps us from always talking, preaching, teaching and discussing the same subject.

Worship can be hindered or helped by the architecture and furnishings of the place of worship. It is good to be deliberate about these when we build churches and decorate them for worship.

Although a recent development in history, hymns are a very important part of our worship heritage. They help us in our praise and thanks to God and in our response to God.

We have realized that ritual is not bad. There are bad rituals, even bad execution of rituals, but rituals are not bad in general. The key is that we mean what they say, and they say what we mean. They are even helpful in public services, in that they help everyone to know what is going to be next.

We have gained new insights into the sacraments of baptism and communion. No, not that we understand it all, nor will we ever in this life, but we have gained deeper insight into their spiritual and physical significance.

We must take a little time for a brief discussion of the order of worship. Some feel that the way to worship is expressed in chapter six of Isaiah in Isaiah's vision. The movement there is as follows: adoration, confession of sin, proclamation of the Word (God speaking) and dedication ("Lord, send me"). Others would say that there are four parts to worship: preparation, proclamation of the Word, communion and dismissal. Those who do not feel that communion has to be served every time would say that there are three or four parts.

It seems to me that a most noteworthy conclusion is that of Robert Webber:

> *It should be noted that the story is more fully told when both Word and Table are the order of service. However, the Word alone proclaims Christ. So on the Sundays or worship times when Communion is not observed, the threefold pattern . . . meets the requirements of Christian worship.*[1]

If Word and table with preparation and dismissal were good enough for the early church, they are good enough for us.

The way we go about doing this is up to us as long as we do it "in spirit and truth."

Final Things

1. **Prepare an order of worship and compare it to your first order of worship (prepared in the first session). Has it changed any? If so, why? If not, why not?**
2. **Please fill out the final evaluation and turn it in before you leave.**
3. **Final prayer together.**

Evaluations

Have course participants complete the weekly evaluation form from page 63 (you may make copies) and hand it in at the end of the class period.

---

[1] Robert E. Webber, *Worship is a Verb* (Waco: Word Books, 1985), p. 64.

Notes

Evaluation Forms

On the following pages are three evaluation forms and one general questionnaire.

1. **The Weekly Evaluation** (page 63) is offered as a regular part of the worship course. It may be used by class participants to be handed in at the end of each class session.

2. **The Weekly Worship Service Evaluation** (page 65) is offered as a supplement to this course. It may be used weekly by class participants. Its purpose is to evaluate the weekly worship service.

3. **The General Worship Service Evaluation** (page 67) is offered as a supplement to this course. It may be used by class participants prior to and at the conclusion of the course. Its purpose is to evaluate individual perceptions of the worship of the church.

4. **The Worship Questionnaire** (pages 69-73) is offered as a supplement to this course. It may be used by class participants prior to and at the conclusion of the course. Its purpose is to evaluate individual perception changes after taking the course.

Weekly Evaluation

For each of these statements circle the number which best represents how strongly you agree or disagree. Number five represents the strongest agreement.

1. The presenter showed knowledge of the subject.   1   2   3   4   5

2. The subject was presented well.   1   2   3   4   5

3. The methods were proper and helpful.   1   2   3   4   5

4. The presenter was sensitive to the needs of the group.   1   2   3   4   5

5. The presenter made the subject interesting.   1   2   3   4   5

6 The presenter was enthusiastic.   1   2   3   4   5

7. The presenter encouraged participation.   1   2   3   4   5

Additional Comments:

Suggestions:

Weekly Worship Service Evaluation

Please circle the number that most clearly rates how you feel. The lowest number represents the lowest rating, and the highest number represents the highest rating.

1. I feel included.	1 2 3 4 5
2. My worship needs were fulfilled.	1 2 3 4 5
3. The service was interesting.	1 2 3 4 5
4. The order of service helped me to worship.	1 2 3 4 5
5. The service was a joyful experience.	1 2 3 4 5
6. The sermon applied to my life.	1 2 3 4 5
7. The sermon helped me to understand Scripture better.	1 2 3 4 5
8. The sermon helped me to live the the Christian life.	1 2 3 4 5

Please check one:
9. The best part of the service was _____.
_____ congregational singing
_____ prayers
_____ scripture
_____ music
_____ sermon
_____ other _____
(explain)

Additional Comments:

Suggestions:

General Worship Service Evaluation

Please circle the number that most clearly rates how you feel. The lowest number represents the lowest rating, and the highest number represents the highest rating.

1. In general on a Sunday morning I feel included.　　1　2　3　4　5

2. My worship needs were fulfilled on Sunday morning.　　1　2　3　4　5

3. The Sunday morning service is interesting.　　1　2　3　4　5

4. The order of service helps me to worship.　　1　2　3　4　5

5. The Sunday morning service is a joyful experience.　　1　2　3　4　5

6. The sermon usually applies to my life.　　1　2　3　4　5

7. The sermon usually helps me to understand Scripture better.　　1　2　3　4　5

8. The sermon usually helps me to live the Christian life.　　1　2　3　4　5

Please check one:
9. The best part of the service was _____.

_____ congregational singing
_____ prayers
_____ scripture
_____ music
_____ sermon
_____ other _____
　　　　　　　　　　　(explain)

Additional Comments:

Suggestions:

Worship Questionnaire

Please place your answer in the blank at the left.

_____ 1. Worship is _____.
    A. done to us.
    B. for us.
    C. by us.
    D. all of the above.

_____ 2. The focus of worship is _____.
    A. the human experience.
    B. the sermon.
    C. entertainment.
    D. Jesus Christ — his life, death and resurrection.

_____ 3. Spontaneous worship services are more filled with the presence of God than are planned services.
    A. yes.
    B. no.

_____ 4. Reading of the Scriptures, singing of songs, prayers and testimonies are preliminaries that lead to the main reason for being in church — hearing the sermon.
    A. yes.
    B. no.

_____ 5. A "real worship service" should include _____.
    A. songs.
    B. scripture.
    C. testimonies.
    D. communion sometimes.
    E. communion all the time.
    F. all of the above.

_____ 6. Church architecture is important.
   A. yes.
   B. no.

_____ 7. The decor of the church is important in the worship service.
   A. yes.
   B. no.

_____ 8. The seasons of the church year _____.
   A. should have some influence on the decor of the church.
   B. should have some influence on the decor of the church and on the worship service.
   C. should have little if any influence on the decor of the church and on the worship services of the church.

_____ 9. The atmosphere of the worship service can work against reverence.
   A. yes.
   B. no.

_____ 10. The church is first _____.
   A. an evangelistic community.
   B. a teaching community.
   C. a fellowshiping community.
   D. a healing community.
   E. a worshiping community.
   F. a mission community.

_____ 11. Worship is _____.
   A. a source for spiritual renewal.
   B. evangelization.
   C. education.
   D. for the sermon.

_____ 12. In worship _____.
   A. God is speaking and acting.
   B. God is bringing to me the benefits of redemption.
   C. God is working on my behalf.
   D. God is repairing and renewing my relationship to Godself.
   E. God seeks me out to bring healing in my life.
   F. all of the above occurs.
   G. none of the above occurs.

_____ 13. Communion is _____.
   A. only symbol.
   B. more than symbol.
   C. the Body and Blood of Christ.
   D. sacramental — a means of grace.

_____ 14. Communion should be offered _____.
   A. every worship service.
   B. once a month.
   C. every six weeks.
   D. every other month.
   E. once a quarter.
   F. twice a year.
   G. once a year.

_____ 15. Art has _____.
   A. no place in worship.
   B. an important part to play in worship.
   C. little value in worship.

_____ 16. Liturgical dance _____.
   A. has no place in worship.
   B. could play an important part in worship.
   C. has little value in worship.

_____ 17. Drama has _____.
      A. no place in worship.
      B. could play an important part in worship.
      C. little value in worship.

_____ 18. Worship _____.
      A. is celebration in our personal lives.
      B. is celebration in our churches' lives.
      C. is both A and B.
      D. is none of the above.

_____ 19. History of worship _____.
      A. has no influence on the way I worship.
      B. would be helpful in understanding my present form of worship as well as those forms of others.
      C. is not important in worship at all.
      D. is of no value at all.

_____ 20. Baptism _____.
      A. is a symbol.
      B. is initiation into the Body of Christ.
      C. is not important.

_____ 21. The mode of baptism is _____.
      A. not important.
      B. to be sprinkling only.
      C. to be pouring only.
      D. to be immersion only.

_____ 22. Infants should _____.
      A. not be baptized.
      B. be baptized.
      C. be dedicated.
      D. not be dedicated.

_____ 23. Baptism _____.
   A. should be done as a part of the worship service.
   B. should be done at special times but not as a part of the worship service.
   C. should be done in private.

_____ 24. Baptism _____.
   A. should be offered at special times in the church year only.
   B. should be encouraged at special times in the church, but available at all times.
   C. has no relationship to the church year and should have no relationship.

_____ 25. Our worship services _____.
   A. are never helpful.
   B. are sometimes helpful.
   C. are usually helpful.
   D. are always helpful.

_____ 26. Our worship services _____.
   A. should be changed.
   B. are fine the way they are.
   C. should be changed once in a while.

Additional Comments:

Bibliography

Abba, Raymond. *Principles of Christian Worship*. New York: Oxford University Press, 1957.

Anderson, James D. and Ezra Earl Jones. *The Management of Ministry*. New York: Harper & Row, Publishers, 1978.

Anderson, Paul, "Balancing Form and Freedom," *Leadership* VII (Spring 1986): pp. 24-33.

Bass, George M. *The Song and the Story*. Lima: The C.S.S. Publishing Co., Inc., 1984.

The Book of Common Prayer. According to the use of the Episcopal Church. New York: The Church Hymnal Corporation, Certified 1979.

The Book of Services. Nashville: The United Methodist Publishing House, 1985.

Bradshaw, Paul F. *Daily Prayer in the Early Church*. New York: Oxford Press, 1982.

Brilioth, Yngve. *Eucharistic Faith and Practice: Evangelical and Catholic*, Translated by A. G. Herbert. London: SPCK, 1956.

Dale, Robert D. *Surviving the Difficult Church Member*. Nashville: Abingdon Press, 1984.

Dix, Dom Gregory. *The Shape of the Liturgy*. Glasgow: The University Press, 1984.

Doran, Carol and Thomas H. Troeger, "Reclaiming the Corporate Self: The Meaning and Ministry of Worship in a Privatistic Culture," *Worship* 60 (May 1986): 3200-3210.

Duck, Ruth C., ed. *Flames of the Spirit: Resources for Worship*. New York: The Pilgrim Press, 1985.

Frank, Jerome D. *Persuasion and Healing: A Comparative Study of Psychotherapy*. rev. ed. New York: Schocken Books, 1974.

From Ashes to Fire: Services of Worship for the Seasons of Lent and Easter. Nashville: Abingdon Press, 1979.

Gesswein, Armin R. *With One Accord in One Place.* Harrisburg: Christian Publications, Inc., 1978.

Guthrie, Shirley C., Jr. *Christian Doctrine: Teachings of the Christian Church.* Atlanta: John Knox Press, 1968.

Hart, Russel M. "Bringing Liturgy to Life." D.Min. Thesis, United Theological Seminary, 1978.

Hickman, Hoyt L. *United Methodist Altars: A Guide for the Local Church.* Nashville: Abingdon Press, 1984.

Hickman, Hoyt L., Donald E. Saliers, Laurence Hull Stookey, and James F. White. *Handbook of the Christian Year.* Nashville: Abingdon Press, 1986.

Hodgson, Peter C. and Robert H. King, eds. *Christian Theology: An Introduction to Its Traditions and Tasks.* 2nd ed. Philadelphia: Fortress Press, 1985.

Hovda, Robert W. *Strong, Loving, Wise: Presiding in Liturgy.* Collegeville: The Liturgical Press, 1976.

Huck, Gabe. *Teach Me To Pray: A Way of Prayer.* Los Angeles: William H. Sadlier, Inc., 1982.

Hunt, Earl G., Jr. *A Bishop Speaks His Mind: A Candid View of United Methodism.* Nashville: Abingdon Press, 1987.

Hunter, Kent R. *Your Church Has Personality.* Nashville: Abingdon Press, 1985.

Jones, Cheslyn, Geoffrey Wainright, Edward Yarnold, S.J., eds. *The Study of Liturgy.* New York: Oxford University Press, 1978.

Kinlaw, Dennis F., *Preaching in the Spirit.* Grand Rapids: Francis Asbury Press, 1985.

Lazareth, William H. *Growing Together in Baptism, Eucharist and Ministry.* Geneva: World Council of Churches, 1982.

Macquarrie, John. *Principles of Christian Theology.* 2nd ed. New York: Charles Scribner's Sons, 1977.

Maxwell, William D. *An Outline of Christian Worship: Its Development and Forms.* 5th ed. London: Oxford University Press, 1952.

Nicholls, William. *Jacob's Ladder: The Meaning of Worship.* Richmond: John Knox Press, 1958.

Ortlund, Anne. *Up With Worship: How to Quit Playing Church.* rev. ed. Ventura: Regal Books, 1982.

Outler, Albert C. *Theology in the Wesleyan Spirit.* Nashville: Discipleship Resources, 1975.

Porter, E.H., Jr. *An Introduction to Therapeutic Counseling.* Boston: Houghton Mifflin Co., 1950.

Saliers, Don E. *From Hope to Joy.* Nashville: Abingdon Press, 1984.

The Soul in Paraphrase: Prayer and the Religious Affections. New York: The Seabury Press, 1980.

Worship and Spirituality. Philadelphia: The Westminster Press, 1984.

Senn, Frank C. *Christian Worship and Its Cultural Setting.* Philadelphia: Fortress Press, 1983.

Stokes, Mack B. *The Holy Spirit in the Wesleyan Heritage.* Nashville: Graded Press/Abingdon Press, 1985.

Stookey, Laurence Hull. *Baptism: Christ's Act in the Church.* Nashville: Abingdon Press, 1982.

Surrey, Peter J. *The Small Town Church.* Nashville: Abingdon Press, 1981.

Sweet, Leonard I. *New Life in the Spirit.* Philadelphia: The Westminster Press, 1982.

Talley, Thomas J. *The Origins of the Liturgical Year.* New York: Pueblo Publishing Co., 1986.

Thompson, Bard, ed. *Liturgies of the Western Church.* Philadelphia: Fortress Press, 1961.

Thurian, Max and Geoffrey Wainwright. *Baptism and Eucharist: Ecumenical Convergence in Celebration.* Grand Rapids: Wm. B. Eerdmans, 1983; repr., Switzerland: Thompson Press (India) Limited, New Delhi, 1986.

Vogel, Cyrille. *Medieval Liturgy.* Revised and Translated by William G. Storey and Neils Krogh Rasmussen. Washington: The Pastoral Press, 1986.

Wainright, Geoffrey. *Doxology: The Praise of God in Worship, Doctrine and Life: A Systematic Theology.* ed. New York: Oxford University Press, 1984.

Eucharist and Eschatology. London: Epworth Press, 1971.

Webber, Robert E. *Worship is a Verb.* Waco: Word Books Publisher, 1985.

White, James F. *Christian Worship in Transition.* Nashville: Abingdon Press, 1976.

White, James F. *Introduction to Christian Worship.* Nashville: Abingdon Press, 1980.

White, James F. *Sacraments as God's Self-Giving.* Nashville: Abingdon Press, 1983.

Wilke, Richard B. *And Are We Yet Alive?* Nashville: Abingdon Press, 1986.

Willimon, William H. *Preaching and Leading Worship.* Philadelphia: The Westminster Press, 1984.

Willimon, William H. *Rekindling the Flame: Strategies for Vital United Methodism.* Nashville: Abingdon Press, 1987.

Willimon, William H. *Remember Who You Are: Baptism, a Model for Christian Life.* Nashville: The Upper Room, 1980.

Willimon, William H. *Sunday Dinner: The Lord's Supper and the Christian Life.* Nashville: The Upper Room, 1981.

Willimon, William H. *Worship as Pastoral Care.* Nashville: Abingdon Press, 1979.

Willimon, William H. and Robert L. Wilson. *Preaching and Worship in the Small Church.* Nashville: Abingdon Press, 1980.

Wise, Carroll A. *The Meaning of Pastoral Care.* New York: Harper & Row, Publishers, 1966.